Original title:
The Monstera Monologues

Copyright © 2025 Creative Arts Management OÜ
All rights reserved.

Author: Riley Hawthorne
ISBN HARDBACK: 978-1-80581-937-0
ISBN PAPERBACK: 978-1-80581-464-1
ISBN EBOOK: 978-1-80581-937-0

The Parable of the Frond

In the heart of the green, a party was thrown,
Every leaf danced, and no one felt alone.
The stems told jokes, twisting in delight,
Even the soil giggled at the moon's soft light.

A frond slipped and tripped on its own weighted pride,
"Who knew plants could party?" the roots teased and cried.
With every leap, the laughter would swell,
In a world of greens, all was merry and well.

Tales from a Hidden Canopy

In a secret nook, where the shadows conspire,
A lizard cracked jokes while the leaves caught fire.
Vines tangled together, creating a mess,
"Don't leaf me hanging!" they each would confess.

Squirrels traded puns, scurrying through,
"Why don't trees play cards? Because they're all too blue!"
Branches above shook with raucous delight,
As the canopy echoed with humor so bright.

Echoes in the Understory

Deep underground, where the roots intertwine,
Worms tell tales, with wit so divine.
"I'm so bored," said one, "Let's start a band,"
The mushrooms all laughed, "We'll lend a hand!"

The beetles all clapped, their shells all aglow,
"Let's make some noise; let's put on a show!"
With a rustle of leaves and a thump of a toe,
Undergrowth giggled, as the fun started to flow.

Leafy Lamentations

Oh, the woes of a leaf when the wind blows strong,
It flutters and shakes like it's singing a song.
"I'm too young to drop, this isn't the end!"
The branches all chuckled, "This breeze is a friend!"

As the sun dipped low, and shadows grew long,
A gathering of greens formed a silly throng.
"Let's sway with our worries, dance with our glee,
For a leaf's a wise soul, and we're wild and free!"

Dialogues with a Dappled Sun

Underneath the bright warm glow,
The leaves chatter, putting on a show.
They gossip on the evening breeze,
Of ants in suits and butterflies with keys.

A dappled sun gives them a wink,
While roots below nod and think.
"Do you see that shadow pass?"
"I hope it's not the neighbor's grass!"

Roots Beneath the Surface

Buried low where jokes are made,
Roots roll their eyes, not afraid.
"Did you hear what the soil said?"
"It's hard to keep my humor fed!"

In the darkness, wise as wise can be,
They plot and plan their bold decree.
'Let's trip a weed or two today,
Just for fun, let's make it sway!'

A Tapestry of Tendrils

Tendrils twist with playful cheer,
In the breeze, they draw near.
"Why did the leaf cross the path?
To find the sun and have a laugh!"

They weave their tales, stories bright,
Of nighttime glows and morning light.
"Let's swing and sway, let's dance around,
We're the funniest plants in town!"

Fronds and Folly: A Plant's Perspective

Fronds discuss the latest fashion,
With rhymes that cause uproarious passion.
"Why wear green when you can wear more?
I'll stick with polka dots galore!"

Chubby stems giggle deep within,
As sunlight beams, their heads spin.
"We'll start a club, no need to hide,
The sillier, the better — that's our pride!"

Echoes of Evergreen

In the jungle, leaves conspire,
Laughter rings from twig and flyer.
A plant's gossip fills the air,
Charming tales of foliage flair.

Vines wiggle like a dancer's feet,
Bouncing to the jungle beat.
Silly critters join the jest,
Sharing secrets, never rest.

A monkey swings, a parrot squawks,
Echoes of nature, playful talks.
With banana peels in a pile,
The palm tree shakes, joins the style.

In shades of green, the fun's alive,
Underneath, the plants all thrive.
A chorus sung by leaf and stem,
Forever friends, the roots extend.

The Heartbeat of the Tropics

Oh, the palms sway with a wink,
Where sun-kissed plants laugh and drink.
The fronds tickle, the flowers tease,
Nature giggles with the breeze.

Coconuts roll like bowling balls,
Falling down with silly calls.
"Watch your head!" the parrot squawks,
Plant parties are the best of talks.

Ferns dance on the forest floor,
While lizards play hide-and-seek galore.
Who knew plants could be so fun?
In the tropics, joy is spun.

The moonlight brings a glimmering show,
As shadows stretch and rhythms flow.
With each rustle of the leafy crew,
The heartbeat of fun resonates too.

Whispers of the Leafy Giant

In the canopy, whispers resound,
A big leaf's tale goes round and round.
It sighs and giggles, rustles and bends,
Sharing gossip of leafy friends.

"Did you see that?!" a liana exclaimed,
"Yesterday's rain, it left me quite tamed!"
The orchids added with sass and grace,
"Just don't ask me about my face!"

With every breeze, stories spread wide,
Of mischievous buds that love to hide.
Banana leaves cover up secrets well,
In this leafy arcana, who can tell?

Yet amid the laughs and playful floods,
Roots tickle softly, bound by the mud.
In this green theater, life's quite the riot,
Where whispers of joy, we proudly invite.

Shadows Beneath the Canopy

In shadows deep, where secrets dwell,
The plants unwind, they weave a spell.
With every leaf, a chuckle grows,
Tales of mischief the forest knows.

Ferns bow down to play and peek,
"Are you in here?" the vines cheekily speak.
Creeping shadows join the fun,
As laughter blooms beneath the sun.

Roots entangled in a silly dance,
Each little sprout takes a chance.
A bumblebee buzzes with delight,
In this leafy realm, all feels right.

So come and sit under the shade,
Where frolic and whimsy are handmade.
In the echoes of laughter, take a seat,
And join the party, oh so sweet!

Eulogy of the Potted Ones

In the corner sat some plants, oh dear,
They lived quite boldly, without fear.
But now they droop, with leaves so sad,
I swear they whispered, 'We've been had!'

With water too much or far too low,
A tragic tale of woe you know.
A spider plant can't spin a web,
Yet somehow caught a damp, dark ebb.

Pothos hung down like a draped gown,
Searching for sunshine, the gleam of a crown.
But found only shadows, while dust bunnies thrived,
These potted ones mourned, yet still, they strived.

So we raise a glass to this leafy crew,
In pots and planters, not much they knew.
Here's to the gardeners, not quite so wise,
May they never forget to fertilize!

The Call of Tender Foliage

Oh, leafy friends, in pots you dwell,
Whispering secrets we can't quite tell.
You stretch and yawn, oh what a sight,
Swapping tales of water and light!

Elegance drapes your vibrant green,
Yet a dust bunny lurks, quite unseen.
'Don't worry, dear! I'm just here for fun!'
You giggle and twirl, bright under the sun.

To fiddle leaf ferns, what's your grand plan?
To snack on sunshine, or just be a fan?
You flaunt your style, with grace and flair,
While pothos just dangles, giving a stare.

So, gather 'round, you quirky bunch,
We'll make jokes over lunchtime crunch.
May the watering cans never run dry,
And may all your troubles just drift on by!

Whirlwind of Botanical Wonders

In a storm of leaves and pots so bright,
We dance through the chaos, what a delight!
Petals flail like the arms of a clown,
In this wild garden, we wear no frown.

A snake plant's strut, so sleek and bold,
It takes the stage, with stories untold.
While succulents sit with their tight-lipped grins,
Plotting great mischief under the skins.

Bamboo shakes chimes in a whimsical breeze,
While cactus holds guard, "Just let me tease!"
We giggle at roots with personalities,
In this whirlpool of green, we find our ease.

So laugh with the leaves, let worries unwind,
In the garden of madness, sweet joy we find.
Raise your pots high, give a raucous cheer,
For every green wonder that brings us near!

An Ode to the Verdant Sentinel

Oh, proud sentinel, standing so tall,
In a world of plants, you conquer them all.
With leaves in a crown, all glossy and bright,
You rule over all, what a wonderful sight!

Your branches sway gently, commanding respect,
While fern fronds giggle, quite looking to connect.
'You'll never be boring!' they cheer with delight,
As you stretch your green arms, reaching for light.

Do the shadows dare challenge your reign?
With smiles in your foliage, you shan't feel pain.
The soil beneath, like your loyal old friend,
Will hold you up strong, through each twist and bend.

So here's to the guardian, lush and divine,
With comedy growing on your leafy vine.
May laughter and sunlight abide on your throne,
In this garden of joy, you're never alone!

Tales Wrapped in Green

In the corner, a giant leaf,
Wonders if it's too much grief.
Grow taller, they say, but how?
I'll just sit here and eat my chow.

A little sunlight warms my face,
Chasing shadows, what a race!
I hear the gossip, oh so loud,
About the cacti and their crowd!

Crickets speak of distant lands,
While I sip nectar from my hands.
Is that a spider in my hair?
Or merely this new leaf I wear?

With twisting vines, I'm quite the tease,
Dancing lightly in the breeze.
A leafy prankster, through and through,
Tales wrapped in green, oh, who knew?

Leaves and Longing

There's longing in the air, it seems,
When I daydream of perfect beams.
Do I want a pot or two?
Why not six? I'll start a crew!

Fiddling leaves, all around,
Poke my neighbor from the ground.
"Hey, Fern, can you come play?"
She sighs, "Just not today, okay?"

Vines entwine with tales galore,
Of adventures just next door.
Is that a breeze I feel, so sweet?
Or is it just my restless feet?

Oh, the lives we grow and weave,
Hoping none of us will leave.
With laughter shared on sunny days,
In leafy hugs, we find our ways.

The Spirit of Slender Stems

Oh slender stems, so tall and thin,
What secrets do you hold within?
With each twist and twirl you make,
Do you plot a plant-based cake?

Bouncing leaves in bright delight,
Dancing through the day and night.
I swear they wink; I see it clear,
Just a bit of leafy cheer!

Whispers shared with bugs and bees,
"Is that a weed?" "Nah, just a tease!"
Growing tall while playing small,
Oh, the wonders we can call!

In the garden, spirits play,
Filling hearts in quirky ways.
So here's to all the plants that thrive,
With every giggle, we come alive!

An Intimate Conversation with Nature

Let's sit down and have a talk,
Between the leaves and on the walk.
Nature whispers secrets low,
With every gust and gentle blow.

"Hey, Tree, why so wise today?"
"I've seen it all; come what may!"
The flowers chime in with their flair,
"Didn't you know? We're quite the pair!"

Roots dive deep to find the fun,
Under soil, we're all just one.
"What's that sounds? A squirrel's decree!"
"Oh, ignore him, it's just his spree."

Buds bloom bright with laughter shared,
Nature's joy is not impaired.
So let us pause and hear the cheer,
In this green world, we're all near.

When Nature Speaks in Silence

In the garden, a leaf leaned in,
Whispering secrets, a gentle grin.
"Why shout so loud?" it seemed to call,
"When all can hear my silence, y'all!"

A squirrel paused, with a sideways glance,
Dancing between branches, it took a chance.
"Is that a plant I see with flair?
Or just a bush trying to wear a chair?"

The daisies giggled, the tulips swayed,
Telling tales of how they played.
"Nature's humor is quite the sight,
With vines that croon and blossoms that bite!"

So next time you stop and stare,
Remember the fun that's hidden there.
In the quiet, nature's got a plan—
A comedy club run by a leafy clan!

The Language of Foliage

Green tongues wagged in the bright sun,
Each leaf chatting, oh, what fun!
"Did you see that bug, all dressed in black?
Thought he was cool, till the raindrops whack!"

The ferns rolled their eyes, tucked in tight,
"Some style is just a silly sight."
But the cacti giggled, with spikes in tow,
"Compare us to you? Now that's a show!"

Laughter erupted from stems and roots,
As vines danced lightly in their boots.
"Who needs noise when we can sway,
Our green chatter brightens the day!"

So if you hear rustling in the breeze,
Know it's plants sharing their little tease.
In the kingdom of green, there's no need to fight,
A leaf in jest can light up the night!

Musings of an Urban Jungle

In concrete corners, plants take stance,
Plotting their plots with a leafy dance.
"A pigeon's coming, quick hide away!"
Whispered the ivy, "It's not our day!"

But on the ledge, a lone flower bloomed,
Said, "Bring on the birds! I'll be consumed!"
With a wink and nod, it spread its cheer,
"Urban jungle? I've got no fear!"

The ferns, they chuckled, swaying with glee,
"Watch out full bloom, it's a bird buffet!"
As laughter echoed through city streets,
Wild talk of petals offered sweet treats.

So if you stumble on a patch of green,
Remember its humor—quirky, unseen.
For beneath the asphalt and buzzing sound,
Lays nature's laughter, joyfully unbound!

Botanical Breathings

Roots wiggle freely beneath the soil,
Sharing whispers in a leafy toil.
"Did you hear that chimera's tail?"
"I thought it's a myth? Let's tell a tale!"

As petals bloomed, with colors so bright,
The garden balled, a riotous sight.
"Let's throw a party, invite the bees!"
"Hopefully, they won't bring the fleas!"

Each vine wrapped tales of sun and rain,
Sharing laughter, joy, and a bit of pain.
"Do you remember that stormy night?"
"A leaf lost the fight, quite a flight!"

So breathe in the charm of plants and trees,
And let their humor carry you with ease.
In nature's realm, laughter blooms bright,
Breathing funny stories from morning till night!

Musings from the Indoor Jungle

In the corner, a pot stands tall,
A leafy giant, it owns the hall.
Friends come 'round, like bees to wax,
They question my friend, "Is it plant or snacks?"

I water it daily, talk to it too,
Hoping it shares some gossip anew.
"What's the latest, all those vines?"
"Who knew houseplants could be so divine?"

Its leaves are big, a natural shade,
I swear at night, they throw a parade.
Noisy with rustles, they dance with glee,
Judging my cooking — how dare they see!

Indoor jungle, what fun you bring,
I smile each day, hear the plants sing!
In this green world, we laugh and play,
Who knew house plants could steal the day?

Echoes of the Tropical Heart

Once a tiny sprout, now so robust,
My leafy friend, in you I trust.
You mimic the sun with your gentle pose,
A wild dreamer, among my toes.

"Patience is key," says the user manual,
But let me tell you, it's quite a kanal!
You stretch and grow, while I just stand,
Contemplating soil with trembling hands.

Comes the day, your leaf turns brown,
I panic and scowl, wearing a frown.
"Did I forget? Was it too much sun?"
You'll bounce back, won't you? Just for fun!

So here we thrive, in our indoor land,
Two oddbods, a plant, and a human band.
In a pot of laughter, we find our way,
Echoes of joy filled with plant-play!

A Leafy Lament

Oh dear friend, you look quite sad,
Your leaves droop low, it makes me mad.
Was it the pizza I spilled last night?
Not your fault, if I'm honest, that bite!

Your green's gone dull, like an old sock,
I swear I checked, just around the clock.
Did I overwater or was it too dry?
It's hard to tell, oh me, oh my!

A little pep talk, that's what you need,
"You're a star! You'll thrive, just take heed!"
Yet here we are, this plant-parent trial,
Life felt easy, now it's a while.

Tomorrow we rise, with soil and sun,
No plant-parent journey is ever done.
If you make it, I promise a treat,
A garden of love, not just bittersweet!

Reflections of a Plant Parent

In my home, a leafy crew,
They laugh and tease, oh yes, it's true!
"Whatcha doin' today?" they seem to say,
"Let's plot our escape, to the sunny bay!"

With watering can, I dance a jig,
While they sway lightly, oh so big.
"Feeding time?" they whisper and cheer,
Buds and blooms, oh joy, oh dear!

I tell them tales of my worldly woes,
As they sip sunlight through their nose!
These green companions, so full of sass,
Do they think of me as the one who'll pass?

Yet here we dwell, a merry crew,
A plant-parent's life is far from blue.
In compost and laughter, we find our art,
Reflections of joy, from heart to heart!

The Pulse of Lush Existence

In corners green, life's wild and free,
A plant tells jokes, it's as fun as can be.
With leaves that sway in a gentle dance,
It makes each moment a leafy romance.

Oh, the sunlight tickles, the shadows play,
This verdant jester finds humor each day.
Roots twist and turn in a comedic flair,
In this jungle circus, there's laughter to share.

When watering time comes, a splash on the floor,
The cat makes a leap, then hides by the door.
Chlorophyll chuckles, it's quite an affair,
In this thriving jungle, care has a flair.

So let's raise a toast to botanical cheer,
Where every leafy friend brings joy, my dear.
In this green realm, let your spirit run fast,
With smiles and giggles, life's moments will last.

Harmony in the Leafy Verse

In the realm of greens, such laughter unfolds,
Where every leaf whispers its secrets untold.
With roots intertwined in a joyous embrace,
Each day is a party, a leafy grace.

Tiny bugs roam like guests at a feast,
So lively, so silly, nature's own beast.
A dance of the ferns, the vines interlace,
In this green verse, we all find our place.

With pots that sway, and sunbeams that laugh,
A plant speaks its truth, the world's autograph.
"Join us," it beckons, "in this leafy spree,
Life's better with foliage and humor, you see!"

So gather around in this natural mirth,
Where plants share the giggles that sprout from the earth.
With harmony found in this verdant domain,
Each leaf holds a story, and joy's not in vain.

Serenity Amongst the Leaves

In a cozy nook where the sunlight beams,
Leaves laugh softly, sharing wild dreams.
With gentle rustling, they sway and tease,
A leafy retreat, where worries all freeze.

Each verdant friend wears a smile so wide,
Plant gossip flows, there's no need to hide.
Petals giggle as breezes rewind,
In this leafy haven, peace is unconfined.

A lizard eavesdrops, a true little spy,
While daisies whisper secrets up to the sky.
Sunflowers grin, they act quite aloof,
Creating a calm with their bright, funny proof.

Serenity reigns in this green majesty,
A leafy tapestry of playful ecstasy.
With nature's own humor, let joys interleave,
In the heart of the forest, we laugh and believe.

Legacies of the Overhead Canopy

Up high in the trees, where the wild spirits play,
A canopy's wisdom makes serious sway.
Its branches tell tales as they twist and bend,
Each knot a memory, each leaf a friend.

When storms roar above, the leaves join a song,
They dance in delight, feeling vibrant and strong.
The squirrels are jesters, leaping with glee,
Nature's comedians in this leafy marquee.

Twilight brings shadows, the stars peek through,
Echoes of laughter in the silver dew.
Ancient whispers of humor linger so sweet,
In this wooded kingdom, where earth and sky meet.

So toast to the leaves, with their timeless refrain,
Where joy finds its roots and makes laughter rain.
In the legacy soaring, let's celebrate free,
The fun in the foliage, for all to see!

Light Through the Forest Canopy

In the heart of the leafy glade,
Where sunlight trickles, unafraid,
A squirrel sneezes, makes a dash,
While vines giggle, a leafy splash.

Caterpillars wear tiny hats,
Debating politics with chubby bats,
Fungi have parties under the trees,
Join in the dance with buzzing bees.

The branches shake with laughter's tease,
As shadows play hide and seek with ease,
A monkey swings, does a silly flip,
While ferns whisper tales with a playful grip.

Here in the mix, where life's a joke,
The trees are wise, but also poke,
They chuckle softly in the light;
Forest fun is pure delight!

Tongues of the Verdant

The leaves chatter as raindrops fall,
Mossy tongues speak to one and all,
A parrot squawks, it can't hold back,
Who knew that grass could talk like that?

Lizards gossip on warm stone,
While flowers smile, their petals grown,
The roots tickle down in the earth,
Sharing secrets of joy and mirth.

The breeze sends a message, a breezy jest,
Dancing grasses put wiggly legs to the test,
A dandelion drifts on a whim,
While weeds throw shade at a sunflower's brim.

Nature's humor, so absurd,
In whispers of leaves and chirps of birds,
A cacophony of chuckles sway,
In the tongues of green, fun's here to stay!

Rhythms of the Leafy Dance

Underneath the wiggly limbs,
Leaves shake like they can't keep in,
A bug leads off with a tiny jig,
While branches sway, hum like a twig.

Cacti join in with prickly flair,
Two-stepping in sun so warm and rare,
Dancing vines curl like ribbons through,
As the forest groves grow lively too.

Beetles roll in, join the beat,
A conga line, oh what a feat,
With every twist, the shadows swirl,
In leafy ballrooms, watch them twirl.

So laugh with me at nature's fun,
Where every plant is a dancing one,
In the rhythm of life, we prance and sway,
In this leafy dance, come join today!

In the Shadow of Green Giants

Beneath the giants, tall and proud,
Whispers echo, soft yet loud,
A raccoon wears a leafy crown,
While shadows giggle, swirl around.

Frog on a toadstool makes a claim,
Says he's the king of funny fame,
With jests that bounce off leafy walls,
Toads in tuxedos join the calls.

The trees shake leaves like a jazz band,
Singing solos on their leafy stand,
As shadows play hide, then laugh and hide,
In the giant's shade, there's nowhere to bide.

So let's embrace the silly shade,
And join the fun they've all made,
In the laughter of giants watch us play,
Life's a comedy show here, come what may!

Soliloquy of the Lush

In the corner, I stand tall,
With a leaf that could catch your fall.
Whispers roll in from the wind,
Is that a secret or just a grin?

My friend the fern, thinks he's so cute,
But I flaunt my style, I bear no dispute.
I watch the humans come and go,
Do they know they're part of this show?

Sunlight tickles, oh what a tease,
While raindrops dance like little fleas.
I stretch my arms to reach the sky,
Is it me, or is this life awry?

The pot's a stage, just for me,
With roots as my audience, oh can't you see?
I'll soak up laughter, growth, and cheer,
For in this jungle, I'm the head engineer!

Secrets in the Foliage

Underneath my leafy crown,
I've seen the quirkiest of smiles frown.
A spider webbed in my green embrace,
Whispers secrets at a leisurely pace.

The bark beetle taps a curious tune,
While the sun dances with the afternoon.
I eavesdrop on gossip, oh what a thrill,
Nature's chatter gives me quite the chill.

Squirrels scurry, looking for snacks,
While I'm over here, guarding my cracks.
The bugs are laughing, what a ruckus!
In my kingdom, we're all quite the focus!

A leaf drops low, ponders the breeze,
Why must we all pretend to be trees?
With a wink and a rustle, we join the spree,
In this leafy circus, just you and me!

Conversations with Nature's Sentinels

Oh, Mr. Cactus, spiney and bold,
You're not getting hugs, or so I'm told.
With a wink I say, keep that prickly air,
Your style is unique, but I do declare!

The dandelions giggle, roots in the ground,
They spread their seeds, without a sound.
While I stand proud, all glossy and green,
What's in a title? You know what I mean!

Bamboo sways like it owns the stage,
Telling tales wrapped up in sage.
We chuckle together, over sunshine and rain,
In this garden of humor, we're all a bit insane.

The ladybug winks, a real charmer,
With spots so bold, but no need for armor.
In the grand tapestry, we weave our tales,
Join hands, leaves, and laughs, as nature unveils!

The Dance of the Green Giants

We're tall and leafy, giants with flair,
Swaying to rhythms, can you hear the air?
The golden sunbeams make our colors pop,
With every green groove, we just can't stop!

Underneath the stars, we twirl and spin,
With whispers and chuckles, let the fun begin.
A breeze comes through like a playful muse,
And we sway in sync, sipping on our juice.

The vines know stories of days gone by,
Of critters and clouds that brush the sky.
Our roots entwined, we form a band,
In this leafy disco, oh ain't it grand?

We'll laugh at the rain, as we jump and play,
Dancing in puddles, oh what a display!
So come join the party, be one of the green,
In our grand dance, you'll find the unseen!

Botanical Chronicles: A Green Narrative

In a pot sits a leafy queen,
With fuzzy toes and a funny sheen.
She wears a crown, a leafy hat,
Sipping sunlight, how about that?

The cactus next door, all prickly pride,
Claims he's the toughest, never must hide.
But just one poke, and you'll likely see,
He's more of a softie, just like me!

A fern named Fernie thinks she's a star,
With fronds that dance, she raises the bar.
But when it rains, oh what a mess,
She flops all around, such leafy stress!

So here in this garden, we live and thrive,
With quirks and laughter, we're so alive.
From roots to leaves, it's a jolly spree,
In this green kingdom, just wait and see!

Songs from the Heart of the Forest

In the heart of the woods, a squirrel sings loud,
With acorn in hand, he's oh so proud.
The sapling sways, joining the tune,
Swaying and twirling beneath the moon.

A wise old oak cracks some jokes on the side,
Claiming to be a tree, full of pride.
Yet when the wind blows, he starts to sway,
Funny how wisdom can flutter away!

The berries blush red, oh what a sight,
Complaining of bugs that buzz in the night.
"Can't a berry chill without all this fuss?
Nature's my stage, but what a big bus!"

In foresty realms where laughter rings clear,
Every creature joins in with a cheer.
A concert of antics, jokes on repeat,
Nature's a show that's a real treat!

The Solace of Solitary Green

A lone plant sits, feeling quite grand,
Whispering secrets that nobody planned.
With leaves held high, it beams with glee,
Not a worry in the world, just it and the bee.

The soil below laughs, tickling the roots,
While sunbeams above strike funny salutes.
This solitary leaf has quite the flair,
Loving its space, with style to spare.

It talks to the shadows, has friends in the dusk,
Sipping on silence, oh what a musk!
In solitude's arms, it finds its song,
And dances with breezes all day long.

So here's to the greens, standing alone,
Building their homes in a world of their own.
With humor and grace, they silently sway,
Making solitude seem like a jubilant play!

Whispers from the Wilderness

In the wild, where the wild things are found,
Laughter erupts from roots in the ground.
A bunny hops by, with a twitch and a grin,
Gentle giggles escape from within.

The brambles all gossip, twirling their vines,
"Did you hear about Fern? She just crossed the lines!"
Whispering secrets with critters around,
In the wild, it's humor that's utterly profound.

A brook sings a tune, splashing with cheer,
Making puns with the rocks, oh so near.
The trees shake their leaves, rolling their eyes,
At the puns from the brook that come as a surprise.

Through laughter and nature, we find our way,
With whispers of joy that lead us away.
Wilderness wonders, a comical show,
Where every giggle makes spirits glow!

Beneath the Plant's Gaze

In shadows deep, I hear a cheer,
My leafy friend stares, always near.
With bits of dust, it's quite the scene,
Expecting me to keep it clean.

As sunlight beams, it starts to sway,
Catching vibes like it's on display.
It whispers secrets, oh so bold,
Of every cat that dared to fold.

Its roots wiggle, they dance with glee,
Sharing tales of old, just wait and see.
While I pretend I know the score,
It's plotting ways to grow and explore!

So here we are, a quirky pair,
Me with my worries, it with flair.
Beneath its gaze, I laugh and sigh,
Who knew a plant could be a spy?

An Ode to the Green Embrace

A leafy hug, so soft and wide,
I swear at times, it's full of pride.
In corners dark, it seems to glow,
As if to say, 'Just let it flow!'

With fronds that wave like hands in glee,
It's cheering for the best in me.
While I make plans to clean my space,
It giggles softly, finds its place.

It listens well to all my dreams,
Befriending hopes in quirky themes.
And if I trip, it breathes a sigh,
"Don't worry friend, just give it a try!"

So here's to you, my leafy mate,
Together we defy our fate.
In every nook, your laughter stays,
An ode to joy in green displays.

The Wisdom of Earth's Greenery

A voice of wisdom in a pot,
Telling me things that I forgot.
Like don't be shy and just have fun,
Or sometimes let the wild things run.

It steals my socks, it knows my style,
A fashion guru with a smile.
When guests arrive and glance around,
It nods, 'Trust me, I'm the best in town!'

With every leaf, a joke to cheer,
It winks at me, "I'm glad you're here!"
And as I water, it sips with grace,
In moments small, we find our place.

So raise a glass to wisdom green,
For all the laughs that might have been.
In plant companionship, I see,
A quirky blend of you and me.

Unfolding the Leafy Tapestry

Woven tales of green delight,
Nature's threads in morning light.
Each leaf a note in giggling song,
Together we laugh, where we belong.

When I forget to water days,
It shakes its leaves, a playful praise.
"Just one more drop will do the trick,
Embrace the chaos, be less thick!"

With every curl, it shows a way,
To spin the dull into the play.
A leafy bard, it ponders fate,
"Embrace the wild, don't hesitate!"

So here's to you, the leafy muse,
In every shade, we never lose.
In laughter loud, we spin in glee,
Unfolding joy, just you and me.

An Invitation to the Living Room Jungle

Step right in, the plants are talking,
They tell me jokes while I'm just walking.
Ferns in frill, so full of sass,
Cacti lurking with a prickly pass.

Here's a party where leaves dance free,
With vines that waltz, as wild as can be.
Laughter sprouts from every pot,
"Water me, please, I'm hot to trot!"

Join the fun, let your hair down,
Spin with the pines, there's no frown!
Silly plants can tickle your heart,
In this jungle, you're a key part!

So bring your jokes, your big ideas,
And let's sip tea, shedding all fears.
In this haven, we'll laugh till we drop,
An invite awaits—you don't want to stop!

The Green Chronicles Unfold

In a pot, a tale often grows,
Of a cactus with feelings, who knows?
He dreams of beaches, warm and wide,
Not prickly fences where he must hide.

A fern with a story speaks of delight,
"Once I danced under the moonlight!
But then I tripped on a loose shoe lace,
And now I'm stuck in this leafy place."

A rubber plant ponders a rockin' sound,
He sways and grooves, never feeling down.
"Join my band," he shouts with flair,
"We'll serenade the ants in the air!"

Together they laugh, in their leafy lair,
Each blossom spins tales beyond compare.
A chronicles filled with humor and cheer,
In this green space, there's nothing to fear!

Tales Tall as the Stalk

Once stood a plant, oh so bold,
With stories of jungles, waiting to be told.
He swayed and giggled under the sun,
"Got a wild yarn? Come on, let's run!"

A succulent chimed in, quite round and stout,
"Short tales are fun, but tall ones go out!
I saw a flower dressed for a ball,
With petals like gowns, she had it all!"

Through soil and dirt, their laughter flowed,
A tale about bugs, how they once glowed.
"Dancing in moonlight, oh what a sight,
A party of plants, all through the night!"

So gather, dear friends, for a tale or two,
In this living room, we'll bid adieu.
To seriousness, let go of all shock,
With stories sprouting, reach for that stalk!

A Symphony of Leaves

Hear the music in the leafy throng,
A symphony born of vibrant song.
Palms play chords, a rustling tune,
While monsteras sway, as they croon.

With every breeze, a melody spins,
Cactus claps, and the laughter begins.
Ferns take lead in a jazzy sway,
"Here comes a breeze, let's dance and play!"

An orchestra of greens, oh what a show,
Roots tapping rhythms beneath the flow.
Petals erupt in joyful cheer,
With serenades for all to hear!

So grab a seat, feel the leafy beat,
With every strum, your heart takes a seat.
In this jungle, where laughter weaves,
Join me now in this symphony of leaves!

The Growth Saga of Stems and Soil

In a pot, a stubborn root,
Tugging hard, it won't commute.
Leavesy wonder, what's the plan,
Shall I grow tall, or stay a clan?

A twisty dance beneath the sun,
Stretching limbs, oh what fun!
Soil's a party, but who's the guest?
Grumpy worms, they poke the rest!

Trading dirt for a fresh start,
Little rumbles, beats of heart.
Falling leaves, a dramatic show,
Time to act, or just lay low?

So here I stand, a stalky lad,
Life is good, I'm never sad.
With each sprout, a new delight,
Rooted fun, both day and night.

Fantasies in Fronds

Fronds are fashion, bold and spry,
Waving gently, oh so fly.
Greenest dreams in a leafy flair,
Every hue, no room for despair.

Twirling like a foliage queen,
In a gown of vibrant green.
Picturing me on a stage so grand,
With a vine's hold, I'll make a stand!

A dance of light, a shade parade,
Letting nature's charm invade.
Fantasies grow, with every twist,
Life's too rich, to leave a list!

Upside down, the petals shrug,
Watch them prance, a leafy jug.
Who needs a crown when you can sway?
In the garden, I'm here to play!

Nature's Requiem

In the garden, whispers creep,
Leaves are talking, secrets keep.
They giggle softly in the breeze,
Nature's humor, sure to please.

Fallen leaves, a crinkled tune,
Dancing shadows under the moon.
A chorus of stems, they croon so low,
Rustle and chuckle, watch them go!

Roots are grumpy, screaming loud,
"Just dig deeper, don't be proud!"
But up above, the leaves embrace,
In this drama, we find our place.

With every season's cheeky jest,
Nature knows how to refresh.
Life's a stage, in soil we root,
Humor growls beneath our suit.

Portraits of Bold Patterns

Splashes of green, spots of gold,
Every leaf, a story told.
In patterns wild, a laugh we hear,
Nature's art, always sincere.

Polka dots or stripes so bold,
Do I wear silk or spin the mold?
With every twist, a playful joke,
In petals' arms, life's a poke.

Beneath the sun, they prance and sway,
Artful madness leads the way.
A canvas bright, so rich and deep,
In leafy laughter, none will weep.

So here's to patterns, bright and loud,
Nature's quilt, a thriving crowd.
Let's showcase blooms, our leafy friends,
In this gallery, the fun never ends!

The Enigma of Green Growth

In the corner, a foliage queen,
Telling tales of what might have been.
With leaves so wide, they catch the sun,
A dance of shadows, oh what fun!

Creeping vines from floor to ceiling,
Whisper secrets, oh what they're feeling.
A curious sprout with dreams so bold,
Wants to be a tree by ten years old.

A cactus thinks it's quite the flirt,
While the fern walks by in elegant skirt.
Yet the bonsai, small and wise,
Gives sage advice with narrowed eyes.

Each morning brings new quirks and traits,
As they gather round for plant debates.
Who needs sunlight, who wants it more?
A giggle fest as they explore!

Portraits of Plant Life

In pots of clay, they strike a pose,
Green and vibrant, nobody knows.
Succulents wink, a cheeky grin,
While orchids flaunt their blooms with sin.

Monocots shout, 'Look at my grace!'
Diverse companions in this leafy race.
Bamboo stands tall, with a holler so bright,
While shadows chuckle in the soft twilight.

A rubber plant with attitude swell,
Shares jokes that only plants can tell.
Foliage laughter fills the room,
While wild berries swoon in berry bloom.

Then there's the ivy, sly and spry,
Creeping close with a winking eye.
'Let's prank the cactus!' it suggests with glee,
And chaos erupts in the greenery.

Vine-Kissed Memoirs

Once upon a shelf, they lived in cheer,
A tangle of vines as friends drew near.
Each tendril tickled the air with flair,
Whispering tales as they swayed in the chair.

A pothos named Jerry, oh how he'd boast,
Of all the sunshines he loved the most.
While a trailing plant laughed, slightly bemused,
It seemed Jerry had gotten quite confused.

A rubber leaf shook with a grin,
Saying, 'Don't worry, just soak in the din!'
With laughter bubbling in all their hearts,
The memories formed like leafy arts.

At dusk they huddled, sharing their dreams,
Plotting adventures that burst at the seams.
A tale of mischief, a shrub in a hat,
'This is why plants are where it's at!'

A Tapestry of Leafy Legends

From jungles deep where legends weave,
Great stories sprout, if you just believe.
The fern recalls a dragonfly,
Who taught it jokes as it fluttered by.

An ancient oak chuckled soft and low,
Sharing yarns of moonlit dances aglow.
While creeping vines formed a chorus sweet,
Singing of friendships their roots would meet.

A sunflower twirled, quite unaware,
That squirrels had hidden acorns with care.
But the secrets of leaves spread wide and free,
Bringing joy to both you and me.

In whispers of greenness, all stories abide,
Of wanderers and wonder, with plants as our guide.
So gather 'round, let the leaf tales unfurl,
In this tapestry of our leafy world!

Reverie in Verdant Hues

In the corner, leaves do sway,
Whispering secrets of the day,
A dance of greens, a leafy jig,
Oh, do they dream of being big!

Potted plants with thoughts profound,
Chat about the sun they've found,
"I want to bask, not just survive!"
They plot their growth, full of drive.

From soil horizons, roots do peep,
In the morning light, they leap,
"Is that a bug? Or just a friend?"
A leafy laugh that knows no end.

With terracotta, they conspire,
Reaching high, they never tire,
"More sunlight, please, just a bit!"
In their green world, they shall sit.

Tales from the Jungle Floor

Beneath the canopy, whispers rise,
Leafy tales of grand surprise,
"Did you see the squirrel's leap?"
In the shadows, vines do creep.

"Oh, what's that thing? A giant pot!"
"Just a garden gnome, not a lot!"
They chuckle soft, in tangled bliss,
Nature's giggle is what they miss.

Pitter-patter, rain does bless,
Each droplet tells of leafy stress,
"I'm thirsty too! Come share the drink!"
In puddles deep, the roots do think.

With every breeze that bends their frame,
They seek adventure, but stay the same,
"Let's tell stories till day is done!"
For in their world, it's all just fun.

The Dialogue of Tendrils

Tendrils twist and intertwine,
Creating chaos, looking fine,
"I'm an octopus!" one did shout,
"No, a snake!" came the leafy doubt.

From windowsills to kitchen nooks,
They share their tales like open books,
"Every morning, I soak the light,"
"But no more than I take a bite!"

They giggle soft when bugs parade,
"Can we have a feast? I'm not afraid!"
A munch of green, then laughter loud,
In silliness, they are so proud.

In pots adorned with tiny hats,
An ensemble of the friendliest brats,
"Let's pose for selfies, quick, my friends!"
In tendril talks, the pure fun blends.

Chronicles of the Houseplant Heart

In a sunny nook, a tale unfolds,
Of rooted dreams and stories bold,
"It's time to bloom, to stretch our charms!"
The peace lilies flaunt their arms.

With dirt beneath, they share great laughs,
Telling tales of sunny paths,
"I outgrew the pot, a rebel move!"
"Now let's dance, let's all improve!"

They sparkle bright in evening glow,
Gossiping soft, their roots aglow,
"Did you hear? The neighbor's on a spree!"
Houseplant tales flow like a gentle sea.

As stars twinkle through the pane,
They dream of meadows, wild and strange,
"Let's have a party, just us tonight!"
In leafy hearts, there lies pure delight.

The Folklore of Fragrant Leaves

In a jungle of dreams, plants wear a crown,
They gossip of sunlight while roots dig down.
With a twist of a vine, and a flick of a leaf,
They giggle in shadows, spreading comic relief.

The ferns tell tales of the snails that parade,
While lilies chuckle at the shade they've made.
Petals whisper secrets with a rustling cheer,
As the breeze joins the chorus, lending its ear.

A cactus in laughter, spikes shining bright,
Tells jokes of its neighbors, a laughable sight.
They prance in the pot, as if they're on stage,
With the sunlight applauding, they grow wise with age.

So here's to the leaves, with a wink and a nod,
In this funny old garden, let's all give a prod.
May their stories grow wild like roots on the run,
In the folklore of fragrance, we all share the fun.

Love Letters to Flora

Dearest Greenleaf, you're a sight to behold,
Your fronds are so lovely, like legends retold.
I send you my wishes on a breeze to convey,
That you brighten my morning, and chase gloom away.

Oh charming Fernette, with your curls so divine,
Each morning I water you; that's love in the line.
Your whispers of gratitude flutter through air,
Each droplet's a love note, a bond we both share.

My sweet Pothos darling, with your tendrils so sly,
You scale up the wall, reaching for the sky.
Let's plan an escape, to the great outdoors,
For frolicking leaves in the sun, oh what scores!

So here's to my plants in this garden of cheer,
With each heartfelt letter, I hold you all dear.
In the ink of my love, may you always remain,
Connected like roots in this greenhouse of gain.

Meditations on Green Beginnings

In pots, where dreams sprout and sunshine does gleam,
The seedlings awaken with whispers of cream.
They stretch up in laughter, toward skies of blue,
Creating a comedy, splendid and new.

Each day brings a dance, a newly found sprout,
As petals unfurl, there's no need for doubt.
In the warmth of the earth, they sway to and fro,
With a wink from a bee, "Let these good times flow!"

From tiny beginnings to foliage bold,
There's magic in growing, like stories retold.
With soil-packed joy, they flourish and thrive,
In this whacky adventure, they're truly alive.

So let's toast to the sprouts, in our garden divine,
Each leaf a connection, a plant-loving line.
May we find in their laughter, the humor we seek,
As we revel in greens, nature's playful technique.

Timeless Connection with Nature's Design

In the realm of green wonders, our roots intertwine,
With laughter as the sun sets, our spirits align.
Each branch and each leaf, a tale to be spun,
In this playful connection, there's joy to be won.

The flowers are winkers, with colors so bright,
While shadows serenade us in soft, gentle light.
With petals that giggle, as they dance in the breeze,
They spin tales of joy, aiming to please.

Through seasons of growth, we twist and we turn,
Learning to laugh, it's our plants that discern.
With every green whiff, we bond and we sway,
Nature's design showing us how to play.

So here's to the foliage, our timeless embrace,
With humor in veins and laughter in space.
Let's celebrate green, as we wander along,
In this garden of jokes, where we all belong.

Celebrations of Sun and Shade

In the sun, the plants all dance,
Photosynthesizing like it's a romance.
Shade is where the gossip flows,
Whispers of the gardener's woes.

Cacti prickle, jokingly,
While vines unwind, grinning with glee.
The tulips tease the daisies bright,
Underneath the moon's soft light.

Butterflies chuckle in the breeze,
Sipping nectar with such ease.
Lively leaves in playful chat,
"Who wore it best?"—the blooms all spat!

Yet as the day turns into night,
They dream of roots and morning light.
A silly symphony, close and bold,
In the garden, tales unfold.

The Garden Club's Secrets

Underneath the marigold hue,
The garden club meets—who knew?
With prunes and shears, they plot and scheme,
Over tea, they share a dream.

"Oh, did you hear 'bout Sue's new ferns?
She thinks they'll dance, but see how she yearns!"
The petunias laugh in soft delight,
As the peonies roll in, quite the sight!

Whispers float on the gentle breeze,
"What's growing well? What brings us peace?"
"Pests and bugs?" they all have fear,
But the gossip makes it much more clear.

Laughter echoes beneath the leaves,
As nature plays host to mischief, it weaves.
Secrets shared among roots and soil,
In this garden, there's much to spoil.

Stories from the Heart of Green

In the heart of leaves, the stories grow,
Of ancient trees and the seeds they sow.
Laughter dances among the vines,
Each twist and turn, a tale defines.

"Once a sprout who feared the sun,"
The elder fern began—fun had begun!
"Now I bask, all arms stretched wide,
Embracing warmth, with pride, I glide."

The daisies share of shimm'ring dews,
While whispering how they've changed their hues.
A sunflower once felt like a clod,
Now it sways, feeling like a god!

As the stories stretch from root to leaf,
Each curl and twist a moment's relief.
In this garden, humor defines,
Nature's tales as bright as the pines.

Chronicles of the Unseen Roots

Beneath the surface, roots conspire,
In tangled tales, they dance with fire.
"Did you hear what happened to Phil?"
A radish whispered, giving a thrill.

"Fell in a hole, oh what a sight!
He asked for help, but not that night!"
The carrots blushed, laughing with cheer,
"Next time, stick to soil, my dear!"

The little sprouts gather 'round,
Exchanging secrets without a sound.
Nourished by laughter, and sunlight's grace,
Together they thrive, in this secret place.

With roots entwined in joyous glee,
They share their lives—so wild and free.
In the garden's depths, their stories bloom,
A hidden world alive with humor and room.

In the Company of Climbing Vines

In the corner sits a vine,
Twisting like it lost its mind.
Each leaf a party hat, it seems,
Throwing leafy wild daydreams.

A rubber plant rolls its eyes,
While the cactus just despises.
"Stop with all the hugging now!"
But the vines don't care, they bow.

A spider plant breaks out in glee,
"Look at me, I'm growing free!"
But up above, the ivy sneers,
"Just wait till I paint you with tears."

The ceiling's just a launching pad,
A leafy contest to be had.
With each new twist a silent cheer,
Vines declare, "Nature, hold my beer!"

The Lilt of Lushness

Green and plump, a floppy leaf,
Sways and dances, oh, so brief.
In the breeze, it takes a spin,
Saying, "Watch me, here's my win!"

Banter amongst the leafy crew,
"Who's the shadiest? You know who!"
The fern retorts, with fronds held high,
"I'm the diva, no need to try!"

A rubber plant rolls in with flair,
"Crown me king, I'm beyond compare."
But the pothos, with its golden smile,
Says, "Come on, let's stay awhile."

In this jungle, laughter blooms,
Underneath all the green costumes.
Each leaf a jester in the sun,
Together, they have endless fun!

Soliloquy of a Spiraling Stem

Twisting, turning, what a show,
A stem that's got the moves, you know!
It talks to the wall, oh so grand,
"Hey there, buddy, lend a hand!"

Climbing high on dreams of light,
With every inch, it takes a bite.
"Look at me, I'm such a pro!
Still can't reach that shoe down below!"

The pot below just shakes its head,
"Go ahead, but don't end up dead."
Yet still it stretches evermore,
Chasing sunbeams, forever sore.

In its dance, it finds a friend,
A trailing ribbon it can bend.
Together they spin, twirl, entwine,
A funny ode to the climbing vine!

Nature's Confessions

In a shady corner, secrets grow,
Plants confide, but who really knows?
"Last week I had a dreadful meal,"
Said the fern, "It was mostly eel!"

The pothos giggled, "Try my stew,
Tastes like sunlight, holds a view!"
But the cactus just rolled its gaze,
"Me, I bask in the sun's hot blaze."

"Let's do a dance," the philodendron cheered,
"Grasshoppers will join, don't be feared!"
Together they danced, nearly lost,
Nature's joy, no matter the cost.

"Like a vine, I confess," spoke the vine,
"Life's a climb, but the view's divine!"
So under the leaves, they share their dreams,
In this green world, nothing's as it seems!

www.ingramcontent.com/pod-product-compliance
Lightning Source LLC
Chambersburg PA
CBHW070334120526
44590CB00017B/2872